Unknown Graves
of
Southampton Township
Bedford County, Pennsylvania

MICHELE L. MILLER

After searching through more than 100,000 online and printed records, including death certificates, obituaries, newspaper articles, etc., I stumbled upon the individuals listed throughout this book. These individuals are most likely buried in a grave with no marker or stone. They may also be buried with only a stone and no inscription. Some may also be buried with a stone or marker that only includes initials.

As always, with this volume of information there is always room for error and I sincerely apologize to the families. Please contact me with corrections or additions so I can make corrections for future reprints.

I spent a great deal of time sorting through records and I hope that you'll find a long lost relative, a mystery may be solved and you'll be able to add another member to your family tree!

For more information on this and other books please visit:
www.southamptontownshipbooks.com

Table of Contents

Beans Cove Methodist Cemetery... 1

Browning Cemetery... 4

East View Cemetery (Chaneysville)... 5

El-Bethel Assembly of God Cemetery... 11

Lashley Farm Cemetery (Elbinsville Road)...................... 12

Mount Hope Cemetery.. 13

Mount Zion Cemetery.. 15

Oakdale Cemetery (Ketterman/Ash/O'Neal).................. 19

Our Lady of Seven Dolors Catholic Cemetery................. 20

Prosperity Cemetery... 23

Wigfield Cemetery... 24

Buried in an Unknown Cemetery 25

Index.. 29

Notes... 32

Beans Cove Methodist Cemetery

GPS Coordinates

Lat: 39° 47' 32.30"N

Long: 78° 34' 40.92"W

39.792306, -78.578033

Address

Beans Cove Road

Clearville, PA 15535

NAME	Infant Child Bridges
BIRTH DATE	December 23, 1925
DEATH DATE	December 23, 1925
MISC. INFO.	Infant Child of Charles Bridges and Anna M. Robinette. Per the death certificate the sex of the child is unknown.

NAME	Infant Daughter Perdew
BIRTH DATE	November 3, 1926
DEATH DATE	November 5, 1926
MISC. INFO.	Infant daughter of Luther Perdew and Elesta Hite

NAME	Conda Boyd Jackson
BIRTH DATE	October 24, 1915
DEATH DATE	December 28, 1915
MISC. INFO.	Infant son of Elisha Jackson and Edith Curbaugh

NAME	Mary Eddy Howsare
BIRTH DATE	
DEATH DATE	January 26, 1950
MISC. INFO.	Information from obituary.

NAME	William L. Casteel
BIRTH DATE	February 7, 1850
DEATH DATE	December 8, 1931
MISC. INFO.	William is buried in this cemetery. His death date is not engraved on his stone.

NAME	Infant Son Bridges
BIRTH DATE	August 6, 1930
DEATH DATE	August 6, 1930
MISC. INFO.	Son of Charles Bridges and Anna M. Robinette.

NAME	Infant Bridges
BIRTH DATE	December 23, 1925
DEATH DATE	December 23, 1925
MISC. INFO.	Child of Charles Bridges and Anna M. Robinette.

Browning Cemetery

GPS Coordinates

Lat: 39° 43' 13.88" N

Long: -78° 33' 05.48" W

39.720522, -78.551522

Address

Black Valley Road

Clearville, PA 15535

NAME	Susan Rachael Bales
BIRTH DATE	July 31, 1865
DEATH DATE	April 14, 1924
MISC. INFO.	Daughter of James Pierce and Mary Jenkins

East View Cemetery (Chaneysville)

GPS Coordinates

Lat: 39° 49' 18.5874" N

Long: -78° 29' 16.008" W

39.82183, -78.48778

Address

Ragged Mountain Road

Clearville, PA 15535

NAME	Clifford Kenneth Perrin
BIRTH DATE	March 16, 1916
DEATH DATE	December 9, 1917
MISC. INFO.	Son of Floyd Perrin and Ada Swartzwelder

NAME	Infant Son Leasure
BIRTH DATE	March 13, 1907
DEATH DATE	March 13, 1907
MISC. INFO.	Son of William Leasure and Amy Clouse

NAME	Infant Daughter Karns
BIRTH DATE	June 24, 1907
DEATH DATE	June 24, 1907
MISC. INFO.	Daughter of Frank Karns and Amanda Grubb

NAME	Emma Wertz
BIRTH DATE	Not known
DEATH DATE	March 26, 1932
MISC. INFO.	Age – About 78 years. Wife of Emanuel Wertz. Daughter of Nelson Ruby and Jennie Twigg.

NAME	Grant Beck
BIRTH DATE	Unknown
DEATH DATE	Unknown
MISC. INFO.	Age – About 62 years. Son of Joseph Beck and Miss Filler. His body was found in a haymow about five miles from his home. Cause of death unknown. He was buried on February 23, 1917.

NAME	William Henry Wright
BIRTH DATE	August 26, 1911
DEATH DATE	August 28, 1911
MISC. INFO.	Son of Henry Wright and Bessie May Imes

NAME	Albert Harris Wright
BIRTH DATE	July 25, 1908
DEATH DATE	June 27, 1909
MISC. INFO.	Son of Henry Wright and Virgie M. Iames

NAME	John Calvin Wertz
BIRTH DATE	February 25, 1918
DEATH DATE	February 27, 1918
MISC. INFO.	Son of John W. Wertz and Rebecca Ellen Bennett

NAME	Emanuel Wertz
BIRTH DATE	November 26, 1844
DEATH DATE	May 8, 1924
MISC. INFO.	Husband of Emma Wertz. Son of Nicholas Wertz and Miss Clouse

NAME	Infant Daughter Stivers
BIRTH DATE	February 26, 1915
DEATH DATE	February 26, 1915
MISC. INFO.	Daughter of Percy Stivers and Amanda Iames

NAME	Ivy Louis Clark
BIRTH DATE	February 1, 1928
DEATH DATE	February 5, 1928
MISC. INFO.	Daughter of Thomas Clark and Vesta Trail

NAME	Chester Earl Adams
BIRTH DATE	July 6, 1904
DEATH DATE	April 8, 1908
MISC. INFO.	Son of Frank Adams and Arena Bennett

NAME	Jane Beck
BIRTH DATE	April 19, 1864
DEATH DATE	February 21, 1940
MISC. INFO.	Wife of Frank Beck. Daughter of Wesley Perdew and Eliza Roberts

NAME	Infant Son Beck
BIRTH DATE	September 15, 1930
DEATH DATE	September 17, 1930
MISC. INFO.	Son of Jay W. Beck and V. T. Bennett

NAME	Hezekiah Bennett
BIRTH DATE	1836 (Exact date not known)
DEATH DATE	May 14, 1908
MISC. INFO.	Married. Son of Joseph Bennett and Margaret Barkman.

NAME	Albert Bennett
BIRTH DATE	September 27, 1878
DEATH DATE	May 11, 1948
MISC. INFO.	Never married. Son of Joseph Bennett and Anna Mariah Johnston.

NAME	Dorthay Rose Bennett
BIRTH DATE	June 21, 1917
DEATH DATE	November 20, 1918
MISC. INFO.	Daughter of Sheridin Bennett and Mary Ann Wertz

NAME	Infant Son Brockey
BIRTH DATE	January 5, 1938
DEATH DATE	January 5, 1938
MISC. INFO.	Son of Chris Brockey and Lula Ratcliff

NAME	Herbert Gerald Browning
BIRTH DATE	July 15, 1921
DEATH DATE	August 28, 1921
MISC. INFO.	Son of Fred Browning and Bertha Swartzwelder

NAME	Brian Keith Bartholow
BIRTH DATE	July 13, 1961
DEATH DATE	July 14, 1961
MISC. INFO.	Son of Zane Swartzwelder and Carol Bartholow

NAME	Infant Son Davis
BIRTH DATE	March 6, 1910
DEATH DATE	March 6, 1910
MISC. INFO.	Son of William Davis and Susie Welch

View from Top of East View Cemetery, Chaneysville

El-Bethel Assembly of God Cemetery

GPS Coordinates

Lat: 39° 49' 4.944" N

Long: -78° 28' 38.352" W

39.81804, -78.47732

Address

3362 Ragged Mountain Road

Clearville, PA 15535

NAME	Charles William Bennett
BIRTH DATE	December 2, 1906
DEATH DATE	January 15, 1936
MISC. INFO.	Husband of Goldie Bennett. Son of Frank Bennett and Virginia Bartholow.

Lashley Farm Cemetery (Elbinsville Road)

GPS Coordinates

Lat: 39° 45' 751661" N

Long: -78° 28' 55.49" W

39.751661, -78.482081

Address

Elbinsville Road

Artemas, PA 17211

NAME	Infant Daughter Vance
BIRTH DATE	August 23, 1933
DEATH DATE	August 23, 1933
MISC. INFO.	Stillborn daughter of Warren Vance and Julia Long

Mount Hope Cemetery

GPS Coordinates

Lat: 39° 44' 56.5908" N

Long: -78° 29' 10.6188" W

39.749053, -78.486283

Address

Elbinsville Road

Artemas, PA 17211

NAME	Infant Son Weimer
BIRTH DATE	March 10, 1907
DEATH DATE	March 10, 1907
MISC. INFO.	Stillborn son of Ira Weimer and Annie Ruby

NAME	Charles William Bone
BIRTH DATE	February 20, 1930
DEATH DATE	March 19, 1932
MISC. INFO.	Son of David C. Bone and May Iames

Mount Zion Cemetery

GPS Coordinates

Lat: 39° 47' 47.1984" N

Long: -78° 27' 6.3432" W

39.796444, -78.451762

Address

Ragged Mountain Road

Clearville, PA 15535

NAME	Jacob B. Redinger
BIRTH DATE	April 24, 1879
DEATH DATE	June 13, 1959
MISC. INFO.	Never married. Son of William Redinger and Barbara Imes.

NAME	Mary Ann Trail
BIRTH DATE	February 18, 1845
DEATH DATE	August 13, 1910
MISC. INFO.	Never married. Daughter of John Trail and Casander Buxton.

NAME	Infant Son Redinger
BIRTH DATE	August 15, 1914
DEATH DATE	September 1, 1914
MISC. INFO.	Son of Thomas C. Redinger and Zella Dicken

NAME	William Erle Redinger
BIRTH DATE	August 9, 1911
DEATH DATE	August 23, 1911
MISC. INFO.	Son of Thomas Redinger and Zella Dicken

NAME	Infant Daughter Redinger
BIRTH DATE	January 25, 1906
DEATH DATE	January 25, 1906
MISC. INFO.	Son of Thomas Redinger and Zella Dicken

NAME	Rhoda May Redinger
BIRTH DATE	December 3, 1892
DEATH DATE	January 14, 1909
MISC. INFO.	Daughter of Thomas Redinger and _____ Smith

NAME	Jasper Imes
BIRTH DATE	January 1, 1859
DEATH DATE	April 22, 1936
MISC. INFO.	Never married. Son of Moses Imes and Amy Bennett.

NAME	Mary Ellen Susan Iames
BIRTH DATE	December 25, 1908
DEATH DATE	July 11, 1909
MISC. INFO.	Daughter of Riley Iames and Cora Meeks

NAME	Goldie Marie Iames
BIRTH DATE	September 27, 1910
DEATH DATE	December 4, 1910
MISC. INFO.	Daughter of Riley Iames and Cora Meeks

NAME	Alvarettie Iames
BIRTH DATE	March 31, 1913
DEATH DATE	June 26, 1913
MISC. INFO.	Daughter of Riley Iames and Cora Meeks

NAME	Faith McElfish
BIRTH DATE	January 15, 1924
DEATH DATE	January 15, 1924
MISC. INFO.	Daughter of Alva B. McElfish and Bertha Pearl Bennett.

NAME	Barbara Fetters
BIRTH DATE	December 15, 1911
DEATH DATE	October 5, 1912
MISC. INFO.	Daughter of Colonel and Rhoda Fetters

Oakdale Cemetery
(Ketterman/Ash/O'Neal)

GPS Coordinates

Lat: 39° 44' 46.158" N

Long: -78° 35' 22.689" W

39.746155, -78.589636

Address

Flintstone Creek Road

Clearville, PA 15535

NAME	Moses Wigfield
BIRTH DATE	April 19, 1839
DEATH DATE	April 19, 1922
MISC. INFO.	Son of Isaac Wigfield. Mother unknown.

Our Lady of Seven Dolors Catholic Cemetery

GPS Coordinates

Lat: 39° 46' 36.1014" N

Long: -78° 36' 3.3042" W

39.776695, -78.600918

Address

Beans Cove Road

Clearville, PA 15535

NAME	Eva Margaret McElfish
BIRTH DATE	August 30, 1882
DEATH DATE	February 24, 1950
MISC. INFO.	Wife of William McElfish Daughter of William James Hollenberger and Mary Ann Barrett

NAME	Charles Conser McElfish
BIRTH DATE	July 11, 1866
DEATH DATE	March 3, 1951
MISC. INFO.	Charles was never married. Son of Norman H. McElfish and Amanda Gross

NAME	Margaret Eva McElfish
BIRTH DATE	August 2, 1916
DEATH DATE	March 12, 1917
MISC. INFO.	Daughter of William F. McElfish and Margaret Hollenberger

NAME	Infant Son Donahoe
BIRTH DATE	April 3, 1929
DEATH DATE	April 3, 1929
MISC. INFO.	Twin Son of Alphonsus Donahoe and Marie S. O'Neal

NAME	Infant Daughter Donahoe
BIRTH DATE	September 14, 1927
DEATH DATE	September 14, 1927
MISC. INFO.	Daughter of Alphonsus Donahoe and Marie O'Neal

NAME	Infant Son Donahoe
BIRTH DATE	January 31, 1926
DEATH DATE	January 31, 1926
MISC. INFO.	Son of Alphonsus Donahoe and Marie S. O'Neal

NAME	Infant Son Donahoe
BIRTH DATE	April 3, 1929
DEATH DATE	April 3, 1929
MISC. INFO.	Son of Alphonsus Donahoe and Marie S. O'Neal

Prosperity Cemetery

GPS Coordinates

Lat: 39° 45' 25.3902" N

Long: -78° 30' 57.6468" W

39.757053, -78.516013

Address

Town Creek Road

Clearville, PA 15535

NAME	Melvin Clifton Vanmeter
BIRTH DATE	January 30, 1925
DEATH DATE	February 16, 1925
MISC. INFO.	Infant son of Clarence Vanmeter and Janie Mace

Wigfield Cemetery

GPS Coordinates

Lat: 39° 43' 42.7578" N

Long: -78° 36' 26.4492" W

39.728544, -78.607347

Address

Street Road

Clearville, PA 15535

NAME	Jamimia Ann Wigfield
BIRTH DATE	November 3, 1847
DEATH DATE	April 19, 1930
MISC. INFO.	Daughter of Henry Bucy and Darcus Twigg

Buried in an Unknown Cemetery

NAME	Elva Mae Roberts
BIRTH DATE	August 21, 1895
DEATH DATE	December 5, 1923
MISC. INFO.	Daughter of L. H. Ketterman and Elva Dolly. Her death certificate states her place of burial as Flintstone Creek.

NAME	Infant Son Roy
BIRTH DATE	October 25, 1938
DEATH DATE	October 25, 1938
MISC. INFO.	Stillborn son of William Roy and Grace Ketterman. His death certificate states his place of burial as Flintstone Creek.

NAME	Doloris Francine Sourbrine
BIRTH DATE	October 7, 1931
DEATH DATE	January 7, 1932
MISC. INFO.	Daughter of Francis Sourbrine and J. Reckrode. Buried in a cemetery in Beans Cove.

NAME	Norman H. McElfish
BIRTH DATE	April 1, 1842
DEATH DATE	March 16, 1915
MISC. INFO.	Son of Thomas McElfish. Mother unknown. He was a widow at the time of his death. Buried in a cemetery in Beans Cove.

NAME	George McElfish
BIRTH DATE	September 18, 1870
DEATH DATE	April 5, 1907
MISC. INFO.	Son of Norman McElfish and Amanda Gross. Buried in a cemetery in Beans Cove.

NAME	Infant Son Oster
BIRTH DATE	March 11, 1912
DEATH DATE	March 12, 1912
MISC. INFO.	Infant Son of Adam Oster and Alverta Ruby. Buried in a cemetery in Beans Cove.

NAME	John Casteel
BIRTH DATE	November 15, 1827
DEATH DATE	November 21, 1921
MISC. INFO.	Son of Archibald and Charity Casteel. He was a widow at the time of his death. Buried in a cemetery in Beans Cove.

NAME	Infant Daughter Casteel
BIRTH DATE	December 21, 1916
DEATH DATE	December 30, 1916
MISC. INFO.	Daughter of Humphrey Casteel and Florence Donahoe. Buried in a cemetery in Beans Cove.

NAME	Christie Ann Bennett
BIRTH DATE	August 1, 1877
DEATH DATE	March 4, 1912
MISC. INFO.	Daughter of Rebecca Ruby, Father unknown. She was married at the time of her death. Buried in a cemetery in Beans Cove.

NAME	Infant Son Bennett
BIRTH DATE	February 29, 1912
DEATH DATE	March 2, 1912
MISC. INFO.	Son of Elwell Bennett and Christina Ruby. Buried in a cemetery in Beans Cove.

NAME	Gilbert Ruby
BIRTH DATE	August 28, 1904
DEATH DATE	September 17, 1927
MISC. INFO.	Son of Charley and Jennie Ruby. Buried in a cemetery in Beans Cove.

NAME	George Marion Bennett
BIRTH DATE	December 11, 1901
DEATH DATE	February 25, 1920
MISC. INFO.	Son of Elwell Bennett and Christina Ruby. Buried in a cemetery in Beans Cove.

NAME	Alverta Ruby Oster
BIRTH DATE	February 10, 1873
DEATH DATE	January 23, 1939
MISC. INFO.	Wife of Adam Oster. Daughter of John Ruby and Catherine Imes. Buried in a cemetery in Beans Cove.

NAME	Charles Patrick Beck
BIRTH DATE	January 24, 1924
DEATH DATE	March 1, 1924
MISC. INFO.	Infant son of Edgar Beck and A. M. Miller. Buried in a cemetery in Beans Cove.

NAME	Infant Daughter Bennett
BIRTH DATE	July 25, 1921
DEATH DATE	July 25, 1921
MISC. INFO.	Daughter of Irvin H. Bennett and Dicie M. Williams. Buried in a cemetery in Beans Cove.

NAME	Herman Guy Ruby
BIRTH DATE	January 15, 1912
DEATH DATE	April 19, 1912
MISC. INFO.	Son of Charley and Ruth Jane Ruby. Buried in a cemetery in Beans Cove.

NAME	Isiah Ruby
BIRTH DATE	
DEATH DATE	April 23, 1907
MISC. INFO.	Age – About 76 years. Never married. Son of Nelson Ruby and C. Twigg. Buried in a cemetery in Beans Cove.

NAME	Infant McElfish
BIRTH DATE	July 9, 1926
DEATH DATE	July 9, 1926
MISC. INFO.	Child of Ralph McElfish and Laura Fetters. Death certificate states this infant was cremated.

NAME	Infant Son Oster
BIRTH DATE	October 4, 1911
DEATH DATE	October 4, 1911
MISC. INFO.	Son of Coser Oster and Kathy Wilson. Death Certificate does not list a place of burial.

Index

A

ADAMS, CHESTER EARL 8

B

BALES, SUSAN RACHAEL 4
BARTHOLOW, BRIAN KEITH...9
BECK, CHARLES PATRICK...27
BECK, GRANT...6
BECK, INFANT...8
BECK, JANE...8
BENNETT, ALBERT...9
BENNETT, CHARLES WILLIAM...11
BENNETT, CHRISTIE ANN...26
BENNETT, DORTHAY ROSE...9
BENNETT, GEORGE...27
BENNETT, HEZEKIAH...8
BENNETT, INFANT...27, 28
BONE, CHARLES WILLIAM...14
BRIDGES, INFANT...2, 3
BROCKEY, INFANT...9
BROWNING, HERBERT GERALD...9

C

CASTEEL, INFANT...26
CASTEEL, JOHN...26
CASTEEL, WILLIAM L..2
CLARK, IVY LOUIS...8

D

DAVIS, INFANT...10
DONAHOE, INFANT...21, 22

F

FETTERS, BARBARA...18

H

HOWSARE, MARY EDDY 2

I

IAMES, ALVARETTIE 18
IAMES, GOLDIE MARIE 18
IAMES, MARY ELLEN SUSAN 17
IMES, JASPER 17

J

JACKSON, CONDA BOYD 2

K

KARNS, INFANT 6

L

LEASURE, INFANT 6

M

MCELFISH, CHARLES CONSER 21
MCELFISH, EVA MARGARET 21
MCELFISH, FAITH 18
MCELFISH, GEORGE 26
MCELFISH, INFANT 28
MCELFISH, MARGARET EVA 21
MCELFISH, NORMAN H. 25

O

OSTER, ALVERTA RUBY 27
OSTER, INFANT 26, 28

P

PERDEW, INFANT 2
PERRIN, CLIFFORD KENNETH 6

R

REDINGER, INFANT 16, 17
REDINGER, JACOB B. 16
REDINGER, RHODA MAY 17
REDINGER, WILLIAM ERLE 17
ROBERTS, ELVA MAE 25
ROY, INFANT 25
RUBY, GILBERT 27
RUBY, HERMAN GUY 28
RUBY, ISIAH 28

S

SOURBRINE, DOLORIS FRANCINE 25
STIVERS, INFANT 7

T

TRAIL, MARY ANN 16

V

VANCE, INFANT 12
VANMETER, MELVIN CLIFTON 23

W

WEIMER, INFANT 14
WERTZ, EMANUEL 7
WERTZ, EMMA 6
WERTZ, JOHN CALVIN 7
WIGFIELD, JAMIMIA ANN 24
WIGFIELD, MOSES 19
WRIGHT, ALBERT HARRIS 7
WRIGHT, WILLIAM HENRY 7

Notes